Marveling

Photographs and Poems of Praise

Jack Perkins

Published by Moosewood Editions
3916 Casey Key Rd
Nokomis, FL 34275

Copyright © 2014 by Jack Perkins
All rights reserved
No portion of any poem or photograph may be reproduced or used without written consent from author/photographer
Except for brief quotations used in reviews.

Moosewood logo by MJP
Front cover by JPWong Designs

For further information on book, poems and photographs, contact "jack@jackperkins.com
Purchase of additional books available through standard online booksellers
Signed and personalized copies can be purchased directly through "orders@jackperkins.com

Printed in China
ISBN: 978-0-692-26710-3

1. Landscape Photography
2. Poetry
3. Nature writing
4. Religion - Spirituality - Christianity

Our lives abound in marvels. Our job is to recognize them, give thanks for them and try to preserve them.

It isn't easy. Too often, memories we wish to keep, escape. Should they ever reappear, it is often to tease us with their fickleness. They are ephemeral, evanescent wisps of color and sound, memory and dream, of voices unheard and places visited. They are the shadows of ouselves.

How blessed, now and then, to be able to glimpse them again if for just a moment. That's what photographs are for. And, for me, the photograph is a voice that speaks in verse.

INTRODUCTION

This is my third volume of Poetography.

Its title came – unknown to him – from our pastor, Chris Romig, in Venice, Florida. Before hearing his sermon one Sunday, I had always used the word "marvel" to refer to a state of mind but not an action. "I marveled at his ability to …" or "I always marvel at how patient my wife is with me …" Now, here was our pastor encouraging us to "Go marveling." Active phrase. Going out in search of the beautiful and praiseworthy, he spoke of as Going Marveling.

Which precisely described what I have been doing for many fulfilling years. Since leaving behind a full-time commitment to TV reporting, anchoring, hosting, and generally splashing my mug on multitudinous screens, I have spent more blessed time outdoors with camera and notebook endeavoring to capture both compelling images and poetic insights. I called my pursuits "cruising snaps." Now I know the right way to describe them.

I've been *Marveling*.

(I marvel that I didn't know I'd been marveling!)

"Poetography" is the word I coined when I started marrying my photography and my poetry, each to complement the other. Not knowing anyone else doing this, all work by one artist, I felt emboldened to make up my own name for the fusion of arts.

My first volume of Poetography focused on Acadia National Park in Maine in whose midst my wife and I lived for thirteen years. It was titled Acadia: Visions and Verse and was well received, credited as Amazon.com's best-selling volume of the year in its category. The images in it were black-and-white, produced in the basement darkroom of a cabin on an island where we were the sole residents. The black-and-white style had been inspired by time spent years earlier with Ansel Adams and had been pursued through several years of dedicated course work with some auspicious instructors at the Maine Photographic Workshops in Rockport, ME..

The second Poetography volume, Island Prayers: Photographs and Poems of Praise came once we had moved to an island off the coast of Florida. It included black-and-white as well as color images taken in many parts of the world.

By now, working solely in digital, I have brought together the results of recent expeditions, many of them with one of the two groups that have become the most influential and important in my professional life.

First is a merry band who began calling ourselves The Six Shooters though the six grew to a dozen or more so, borrowing a technical photographic term, we playfully renamed ourselves "The Circle of Confusion." It's a privilege to travel with these chaps as they include some of the great photographic minds and artists including digital photography's pioneers and chroniclers.

Other travels have been with another companionable cluster, eight of us, some painters (including at least two of international renown), and some photographers. Given this combination, photographers and artists, we decided to bond ourselves as a formal if unruly organization, to travel together in pursuit of our arts and to be known, ever after, as The Phartists. One of our members sketched a logo for us that we quickly had embroidered on shirts, caps, vests and printed on business cards.

Traveling together, four couples (and we long since decided that eight is all we'll ever be; only charter members to be admitted) we find ourselves learning from each other, sharing between disciplines. If one of the artists is taken by an image made by one of the photographers, there's no hesitation letting him or her use it as reference for a painting. We appreciate each other's work and enjoy each other's company. That's not unimportant. If you're seeking to capture beauty, it's best to have a beautiful time doing it.

A final, personal word. Among the artists with whom I travel, some are ardent believers, some are doubters and some total dismissers of faith.

A reader of these pages will have no trouble placing me on the continuum.

Jack Perkins
Casey Key, Florida

Marveling

Let us now go marveling
Discovering joy-jewels hidden from ken
Wonders wondrously recondite
<u>Mirabile visu</u> but seldom beheld
I find as I indulge my eld
'Tis God provides each great delight
If fed only morsels made by men
My soul would be a starveling

So marveling we now shall go
Pack well. Remember we shall need
To bring along such blithe belief
As alone understands that amid life's prose
Awaits a poem in repose
We, by losing ourselves in a leaf
And taking the time its poem to read
May learn to believe what we'll never know

ZARATHUSTRA MOMENT

Don't be still in bed, undressed
When it's time for the sun's resplendent display
It rises to tell you you're being blessed
With another chance to set things right
To shed the doubting shroud of night
And brighten along with the brightening day

So out you should be on a seaside swing
Swinging and feeling the morning lift
Inhaling the scents the breezes bring
Noting the mellowing hues of the sky
And telling yourself how favored am I
To be given -- once again -- such a gift!

Morning Bird

Fly
Morning bird
Fly across the sun
Take its light upon your wings
Carry it to people near and far
Who, whether or not they know it, need the light
(Those who have the greatest need can be the least aware)
The same it is with the gifts of God; if someone does not share
His light with others, dark will be their night
Many unenlightened souls there are
Who do not know the King of Kings
So who must be the one
To spread the word?

Honeymoon Cottage

When built, it was called the Honeymoon Cottage
A stilted haven for a new-married couple to share
Set apart as though afloat with a shielding sea
As its moat, assuring the lovers their privacy there

What an ideal refuge! As long as the sea protects
Ah, but sea holds sea-crets and winds conspire
And storms erupt one after another as happens
With marriages themselves; storms come, they expire

Honeymoon Cottage tried through buffeting storms
To survive, but wedding vows are only words
Time came the honeymoon was over, the stilted
Cottage ruins abandoned to birds

The First Step

If you come to the place at just the right moment
On just the right day
In just the right season
Of just the right year
There beckons a Spielberg fantasy

You know, you just know, that should you choose
You could walk that glowing dock
All the way to the sun
Anyone?

Don't let Icarus say you nay
Scare you away
His was a different fantasy
This one is yours
He was fleeing imprisonment
You are simply marveling

Ah, but you ask, how many million miles
All the way to the sun
Surely too far, surely, you say
But no! In fantasy distance is not --
For a marveler, miles melt
Take a step and you are there
It couldn't be easier
You just have to take the first step

Eye of the Sky

Oh, but if I, with the eye of the sky
Could see how all began
Could feel the elation
The burst of creation
The molding from mud of man

Woman from rib
The snake, the fib
Man and woman deceived
(Or am I a dope
With less sense than hope
To believe what should not be believed?

Dogmatic cosmologists
Astro-geologists
They write the gospel today
Biased biologists
Arch archeologists
Hark to what they have to say

They say religion's for gullible pigeons
God is a human conceit
They worship pagans
Darwins and Sagans
And nature whose singular feat

Was when natural law
Which they hold in awe
Created, they say, everything
No deity needed
No god interceded
Nature alone the king

Which would mean to begin
That there is no sin
No rules, no right or wrong
No meaning at all
Behind the call
Of the loon or the warbler song

No purpose to life
To husband and wife
To the Christian worldview
The Christian-Judaic
Moral mosaic
Is void if what they say is true

But they don't know
They postulate so
And trust we'll believe what they say
But for me, if I must
Be expected to trust
My trustees will not be they

I'll not place reliance
On dubious science
There's something beyond the facade
Science's libel is not my bible
My Bible was given by God

The Darwins and Sagans
And all of the pagans
Who claim I am kin to an elephant
The more they misknow
The more they show
That not God but they are irrelevant

People of the Steeple

How inspiring the spires that people
Of faith erect when they found a town
Building a church and lifting a steeple
To beckon the faithful from far around

Both steeple and their hearts they raise
While letting hearty voices fly
To fling their Alleluia praise
Up toward the pastel-ribboned sky

Up to that gleaming if ill-defined place
They allegorize that heaven must be
(Though they know it is merely astral space
Stretching incomprehensibly)

Thus, in a word, is the puzzle defined:
Incomprehensibility
Mortal men of mini-mind
Unable to grasp what they cannot see

And so they conjecture a Heaven place
To which, one day, they hope to repair
And meet their Maker face to face
(If by then meet their Maker they dare)

A Simple Church

It isn't much
It needn't be such
An elaborate edifice, stained glass and gilding
Marble turrets, a rococo building
Designed to impress, though not to touch

The heart or soul. Not one of these
The people here are simple people
Happy with a simple steeple
Asserting itself in spite of the trees

As toward the sky their steeple lifts
A call to all from all around
To come unto this holy ground
And receive a simple church's gifts

Then and Now

They were buried here so long ago
Who, today, remembers?
Does anyone, anymore, care?
Why are they here?
They, of course, aren't they.
The they of them long since departed
What is here, moldering 'neath
ramshackle slabs
Is something other than they.

Slabs, tended, can be dearly remindful
Though at this Newfoundland church
They seem no better tended than attended
Perhaps because by now
There are more folks out here
Than in there.

In there
The building is large. A rustic glory
But it's people are few
Growing fewer.
From pulpit, eloquent homilies flow
The word still goes forth
But to whom?
To whom?

A Homonymic Homily

What need for stained glass at such a site
When the sight at the site is enough to excite
And inspire
All who aspire
Hearts afire
To reach even higher
Than Teton spire
What need for stained glass?
What need for choir
When bell is tolled
And truth is told
And God extolled

When each one prays
His praise aloud;
Only praise allowed
By radiant cloud
Where every peek
At mountain peak
Effects to pique
The reverence of which I speak

I look on this scene
That few have seen
And pray that the sight at this site I cite
May incite
Insight

The Unbeliever Speaks:

Look! Isn't this one of those places?
Clubhouse for pretending saints?
People who paint sincere on their faces
And raise to their deity niggling complaints
That they think He should promptly redress
They beg and beseech the most trivial boon,
Devoutly expecting nothing less
Than what they demand -- and expecting it soon.

To the Clubhouse they come when it's time to grieve
Reciting prayers sanctimoniously
They say they are sinners (though they don't believe)
They believe that they are more righteous than we
Talking of tithing's a favorite game
How much of their fortunes to allot
"Ah, but God will provide" they proclaim
Assuming thus that they need not
They know that they are assigned to invite
The "unenlightened" of every station
To join them in the Holy Light
Yet they live in the dark of their own illumination

Is church today little but shallow self-love?
Is that how the faithful have become
As their dearly safeguarded freedom _of_
Religion has become the freedom _from_?
Their nation, they thought was a Christian Land
But now they're told that's no longer true
As the numbers of us, out here, expand

Parable

Preacher telling a parable said:

Was a place for children able to hear
But, neurons miswired, not understand
Was a teacher, spent and hiding a tear
As with all the patience at his command
He tried one last time to reach a dear
Little girl, gently taking her hand
"And how was Thanksgiving at your house this year?
Turkey and pie? Was the meal just grand?"
Beaming, she answered, *"My shoes are red."*

Preacher continuing parable said:

Was a church I attended, a service that soared
The choir, each anthem a holy cheer
The organ, majestic, chord after chord
And then the sermon, simple, serene
The pastor given the voice of the Lord
And I knew, as it ended, that God was near.
But so was my pew-mate who getting up roared:
"Think the Packers'll make the playoffs this year?
That's what he said: *"My shoes are red."*

Inspired by a story told by Pastor Fred B. Craddock

Cold

I can't remember ever being so cold!

You can't? Try. Try to remember your days
Of discomfort, of danger, the terrible times of trial
When chilling specters of peril precluded a smile
When you felt yourself rigid with fear like the icy displays
On an Idaho mount. Try. These are tales to be told

At long-after huddles when yarns of courage are spun
And you spin your own and even embroider the tale
Of flash-frozen mummies on wind-torn hill and you
Locked in that gelid hell, no way to subdue
Only to be subdued -- so you regale
The crowd wants to hear more but with that you are done

Your time in gelid hell is a tale to be told
But also a test. You may shy from tests but shouldn't
You need them in order to grow. You cannot count
Yourself complete until you've climbed your mount
That frozen, windy peak you thought you couldn't
And still can't remember ever being so cold

You suffered but you also learned to cope
With suffering and grow through times of stress
As Paul, in Romans, wrote his adherents
Suffering produces perseverance
Perseverance, character; and, yes
Character, in turn, produces hope

Sperm Whale

With flying flukes and massive muscled girth
This modern Moby Dick, majestic whale
Looms the most ponderous predator on earth
With the largest brain of any creature -- tail

That can power him down a mile deep or two
To devour giant squid, his favorite food
To stay for an hour or more and surface to do
What a newly-fed has need to do, then, breath renewed
Dive, affording this final view
It's only a glimpse but we marvel in gratitude

Twillingate

The waterfront at Twillingate, Newfoundland
Reflects the circumscribing patterns of our lives
The verticals that oftimes aren't
Horizontals and obliques
Angles -- acute, obtuse
Superimposing one on the others
Walls and fences
Pilings and shingle rows

An artist coming upon the scene
Would shy from painting such tangled perspectives
While, unknowingly, living a life
No less recondite

Windows

Some people think that windows are a sighted buildings eyes
With which the building looks at -- other buildings I surmise
But could it be that blithe conjecture might be upside down?
Perhaps it's time to think of things the other way around
That eyes are people's windows; other people looking in
Can see if we are occupied
Or vacant once again

Cunningham's Cabin

How the winds must have wailed through the chinks in the cabin
Wild, wintry, Wyoming winds
Knifing, cutting, likely depressing
The huddled, shivering clan
Children, woman, man
Enduring hardships they perhaps did not think as hard
For this was what they knew
This, and I like to think, one thing more
They knew their Lord
Knew that He would always accord
For every seeming hardship
Meet reward
For screaming, slashing winds
The dazzling, healing, holy view
For suffering cabin-bound mortals
Mountains, their snowy nimbi lighting the way to belief

Were those enough back then for the Cunningham Clan?
Would those, today, suffice for me?

OLD BOARDS

Old boards bend and tend to shrink
Buildings sag and, sighing, settle
Does that mean we should only think
Of how they were in finer fettle
Pretending no change do we observe?
That does them no honor; they may be robust
No longer but proud and willing to serve
Until the time of dust to dust

Old bones bend and tend to shrink
Bodies sag and, sighing, settle
Does that mean we should only think
Of how they were in finer fettle
Pretending no change do we observe?
That does them no honor; they may be robust
No longer but proud and willing to serve
Until the time of dust to dust

Ritzy Reflections

Some of us care more how others reflect us
Than how we really are
In order to be what others expect us
To be we have to star
In a parody under another's direction
A part that never fits
For God didn't make us to be reflections
He made us to be the Ritz

Considering Trees

Bending to the storm

Southern Drawl With Moss

200 YEARS 200 FEET

MOON CHAIR

CALL ME JOSHUA

Reaching

One spring in the meadow, one long ago year
Sap would not pulse through the old tree's core
Nor vernal buds of leaf appear
Nor sweetening blossoms; never more
Would romping child or browsing deer
Savor the fruit of its bountiful store

Yet still it would stand, that derelict tree
Survivor hardly surviving, yet each
Passing season there it would be
Fingering upward as though to reach
To the maker of trees (the maker of me)
What a lesson this patient tree has been teaching
I pray, my time come, I too will be
Still reaching
Still reaching

Kneeling Tree

What a storm it must have been that day
Forecasts for Apalachicola
Didn't say nature was about to unroll a
Juggernaut of wind beyond control, a
Person wouldn't know.
But did the tree know so?
Is that why it kneeled to pray?

It had taken all the precautions it could
Driven its roots deep in the earth
Still, come the day the skies gave birth
To a tempest that raged for all its worth
And clawed away the shore
More, then more and more
And, please, a tree is only wood

The supplicant lost its fervent appeal
That's no guarantee for man or for tree
Even those who kneel

OLD TREE IN FLOOD

No need for color in the scene
To illustrate the sturdy truth
A drownéd tree submerged in flood,
Feet embedded now in mud
And the tree itself, no longer a youth
Snuggles a promising shoot between

Its roots, giving succor for it knew
Well how it feels for a sprout
To face it's first flooding alone,
No one to guide it, on its own.
The old tree knew how it feels without
A friend. I pray you never do.

ALONE DOESN'T HAVE TO BE LONELY

At times I needn't see a tree
To see a tree

The same with God and me

OVATION

Nothing to be said; no use for words
Before I even mutter once
God preempts my utterance
And I, in silence, marvel at the birds

Swans where normally they aren't or meant to be
Freshwater creatures afloat in the salt
It isn't anybody's fault
They seem content despite the anomaly

I wonder: Could this be an incarnation?
Not for the first time, Spirit as bird
That proudly delivers the unspoken word
Then gives either me or himself a standing ovation

Omigod!

The whisper-gasp escapes unbidden
As I turn on a drizzly morn and suddenly see the 'bow

Omigod!
Careless profaning that quickly resolves into resolute, whispered prayer

Oh, my God! My God!
How sanctifying this sodden day
To behold before me
In sunlight shattered, hues arrayed
The arc of your covenant
Pledged anew
I came this morning to see if I could apprehend
In a moment, a bit of the beauty
That for Paul was proof sufficient

I came to capture an instant
You gave to me Yourself

Vision

If I trust my eyes
Wispy waters fall in the distance

If I look with my heart
Gazing deep
Angels dance

Moonset

Sunrise and sunset get the attention
(The flashy always do)
People rise early to capture the hues of the rise
They come back late hoping, so they say
To spy in the sky the rumored green
(The flash that never does)

Sunrise, sunset
They get the most notice
But for me, I'd rather the moon
Unflashy, mellow
A full moon unrolling its carpet of light across the water
To illumine the groins and morning bird
Lighting as well the morning hope in my heart

Too Perfect

Measured minds of men want order
Precision
Things, if not symmetrical,
Tidy at least
So farmer-captains march their trees
Out in close-order drill
Deploy their crops in fastidious rows
And for naught

Anyone passing knows the ruse
That here is nothing natural
It is mind-bound men vainly attempting to improve
That which does not need improving
Nature does not require order
Or what men think as perfection
In chaos too God can work

Psalm of the Rolling Fields

Rolling green and ripe, a gravid earth
Prepares to bear her fruit, spread her seed
The annual parturition for which she will need
The help of many midwives to attend the birth

Those who are called to toil from dawn to dusk
Praying for needed rain; preparing for drought
In good years living with; in bad, without
Their lives sometimes the kernel, sometimes the husk

We story these such stalwarts and rightly enough we should
But they're just the midwives; more, we should honor the mother
Earth. And most, revere the Ultimate Other
Psalm of the Rolling Fields: God is good

Everyday

I choose, along with Emerson
To value most the quotidian truths
Instead of the ever-rare aurora
For me, it's a melting dawn that soothes

I don't need majestic mountain peaks
Puffy quilts of hill suffice
If a pickup on its morning rounds
Raises a curtain of dust I think: How nice

Nice is enough for me, you see
No need at all for the unwonted stunt
Of nature -- the once-in-a-lifetime sight
No. The wonted is all I want

The ordinary, commonplace
In those. lives Him to whom I pray
With faith in Him I'll contentedly fill
My every day -- with the everyday

Rape

Sometimes nature can simply stun
As when I am led to a rendezvous
With a single field of ripening rape
Glaring yellow as the sun
Umbrella'd by improbable blue
I look upon it, mouth agape

Stricken by startling splashes of hue
No adornment do I need
Just primary color on primary color
Brilliant, dazzling, blinding view
Those who this spectacle fail to heed
Their vistas and lives are that much duller

They who look upon the field
And see but another crop to tend
Seed to harvest and crush to oil
So many acres, so much yield
Cycle of labor, never to end
The field, their world of tedious toil

They need for a change to squint their eyes
And see but a blur with no detail
And in that blur find one thing true
And simple that will let them rise
On wings not their own and sail, sail
Through sunburst yellow and improbable blue

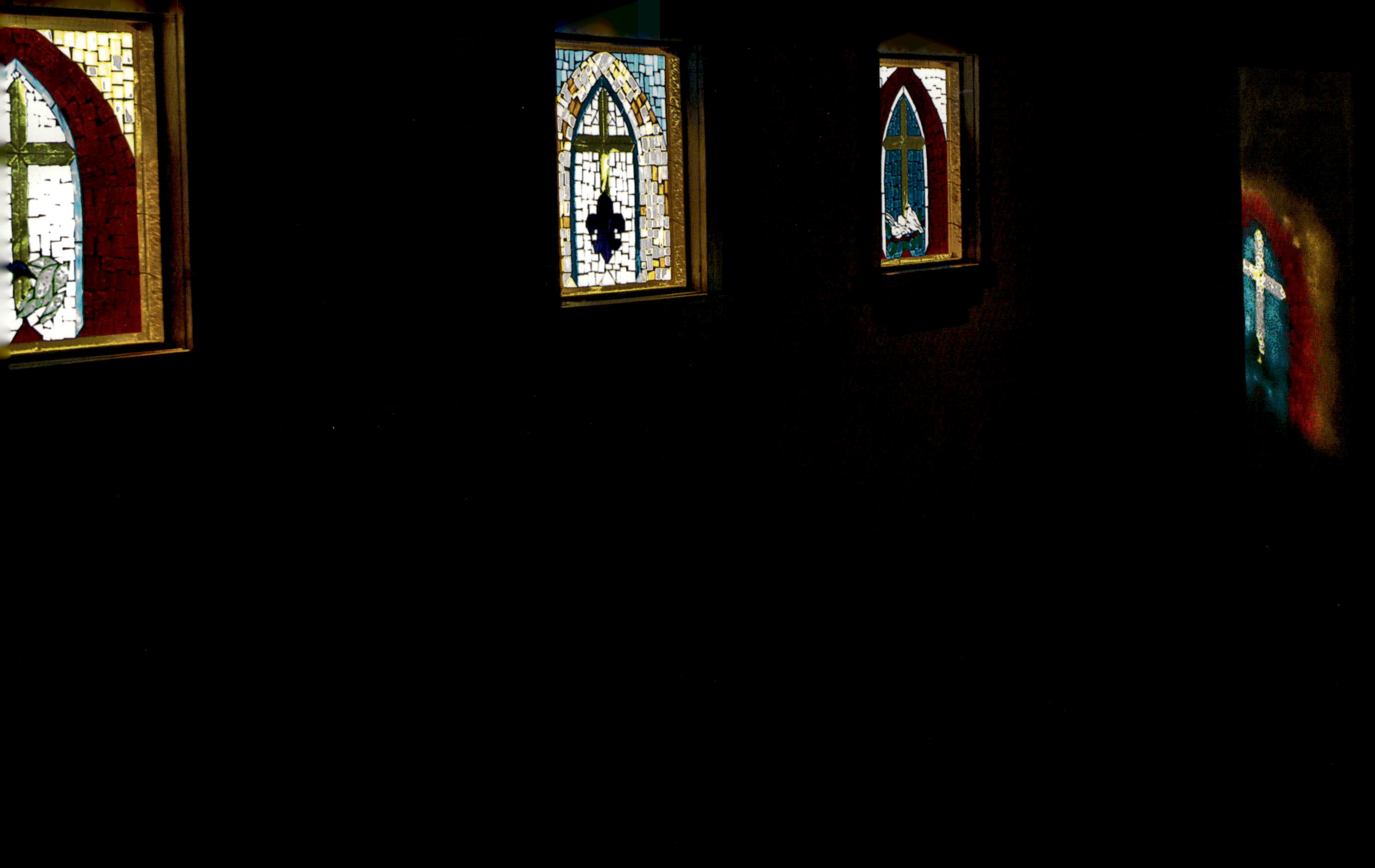

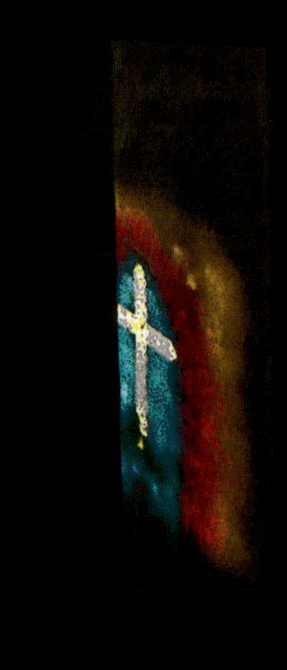

The Gaudy / The Godly

El Santuario de Chimayo
Offers, if I let it, a homily unspoken
A sermon in bright and dark
First, it draws my wandering eye
To that which should not be first
Drawing to dazzle
Luring to light
I stare at the brilliant stained glass
Stare and study
Only slowly and vaguely intuiting
That there is something awry

Each window should be projecting
Its dancing light onto walls across
But no! Stare longer, study the sights
It is peculiar about those lights
Not one of the light medallions on walls
Matches any one of the windows
Puzzled, intrigued, and wholly bedazzled
I realize I am being deluded
Perniciously misled
(How often it happens
Our attention commandeered?)

In this case, the thief is light
Light that tugs me inexorably away
From that which is hidden off in the gloom
The gaudy obscures the Godly

Believer in the Desert

I knew not what to expect when I came
To the desert with friends from across the land
Believers and non-, theists and a-
Out each morning to waken the day
Calling its colors to splash on the sand
The sun to patiently reclaim

Its rightful role -- but not just yet
Let light stay warm and shadows long
As photographs and memories
Are caught and fixed. Then, taking ease
Each can lift up each's song
Of praise or denial; doubt or debt

Actually there is no doubt
No doubt expresssed as we share the morn
Believers don't doubt to whom debt is owed
Who, upon us these gifts have bestowed
Who created the scenes that adorn
Our lives, ourselves, within, without

Unbelievers don't doubt; they trust in the known
Facts from electronic library shelves
(How impoverished lives cirumscribed by the act
Of trusting only provable fact)
Worshipping knowledge they worship themselves
They, their own idols, they alone

For myself, I can't conceive
Of being left without the glow
Of understanding that evevything I'm seeing
Is testimony to His being
Let others believe in what they know
I know what I believe

Desert new Desert Old

Sand that has never known a sea
No beachwalkers padding happily
Only pastels of aridity
Only life that prickles and stings
Creeping, slithering, biting things

But then, as though to make all right
Dizzily dazzling desert blooms
Growing here so one assumes
To be the melodies of grace
In otherwise a tuneless place
Space of sallow, subtle hues
(Did nature fail to get the news
That bright and splashy are the way
The world prefers its palette today?)

But forget today, think of a time
Millennia past in a distant land
No cactus there but lots of sand
And men the world thought as lowly
But it was in them that grew a holy
Faith that supplanted a culture of many
Gods where men could worship any
God he thought to be most giving
With a culture of only a single living
God -- El, or Elohim
Many ways to speak of Him
Once as desert years went by
Men spoke of their God as El-Shaddai
Or an unpronounceable tetragram
Till finally God told them "I am --

I AM

This happened in desert such as I slandered
Before as bleak and tuneless land
But tunes that arose in those ancient days
Are now the historic hymns of praise
We sing remembering Abraham
And the desert that introduced us to

The great **I AM**

I AM

Is who He is

What I am

Is what I need to learn

Glimpse

*So this is what it looks like
The roof of the world
Golden
Just as I thought it would be
How, in fancy, I dreamed it*

*Below, spreads the earth
Yet, it would seem, unpeopled
Virgin
Still imagining Genesis*

*And above it all
What rises above?
Ah, for now, dear friends
We get but a glimpse*

How peaceful Helen looks from here
From now

But <u>THEN</u> . . .

Jackstraws

More than three score years ago it was
The day the mountain blew
Forces primeval, forces evil
Exploding in fiery, liquid rock
Blasting furnace winds that raged
Three hundred miles an hour
Hurricane times two
Ripping, stripping that for miles around
Forests mature were felled and strewn
Stripped to whips
Scattered about like pickup sticks
With no one to pick them up

Today those barren poles, tumbled jackstraws
Pose a question unanswered

God made the forest
God made the mount
God made us to witness
How one took the life of the other
Why?

Mt. St. Helen's haunting enigma

BISON BISON BISON

Original American
Former owner of the plains
Once he ranged in myriads
Of which but memory remains

Today, to guarantee all eyes
All minds, all focus be on him
The overtowering mountains deign
To shroud themselves behind a scrim

So that he alone in ragged robe
Shakespearean, commands the stage
Soliloquizing in the mist
This icon of another age

Buffalo, some people say
Who haven't checked the formal list
For "bison bison bison" decreed
A stammering taxonomist

A treble name to comprehend
This ponderous ton of antiquity
Yielder of meat, provider of warmth
And occasional iniquity

This greatest beast is more to be feared
By man than wolf or cat or bear
And yet, yet, something happens that day
I think it happens. Let me share

I step from behind the camera and climb
The grass of his hill, an exercise
That brings me gazing into his gaze
Those knowing orbs, those ancient eyes

I grasp his horns and slowly lower
My forehead to his; he does not stir
Neither of us is surprised as it happens
Cool skin laid upon warm fur

The steam of his breath moistens my face
I inhale the damp and close my eyes
Close my eyes -- and yet still can see
Though not as before and I realize

No longer am I, without, gazing in
But somehow I am within seeing out
Seeing as he sees. How can that be?
I don't understand but do not doubt

I sense in my sinews confounding truth
That a transformation has begun
I am now he, looking down, seeing me
And we are kin, and we are one

Raising my gaze to the milky sky
I see no shape or form or face
And yet I know it, know that from it
Somehow I feel comfort. Place

Me on my hill in a meadow
Or out across the plain and I
Will always be connected to
The power of that milky sky

It gives me freedom, finds me grass
Gives me all I know as real
I guess it even provides this most
Peculiar feeling that I feel

No longer cool skin against my fur
That's not what I'm feeling now
I'm feeling strange and yet familiar
Warm fur beneath my brow

Releasing the horns, I raise my head
And there again are those ancient eyes
Ponderous One and Ponderer
Each the other in disguise

O am I daft? Was it all chimera?
You say transmigration can't be?
But I insist. And remember a group
Of us bison is called an <u>Obstinacy</u>

THE DEEP WOOD

Dappled and dear
Never out of its mother's sight
A yearling gambols somewhere in the wood
The deep wood

Light chases dark
Blots of shadow, flashes of sun
Dance about the mossy knots in the wood
The deep, mottled wood

There is a thrush within
A bird we are blessed to hear
Truth told, it is not much to see
But, oh, it is much to hear
As it tootles its liquid flute
Unseen in the wood
The deep, mottled, melodic wood

Should you one day choose to step through
The frame and into the wood
(And you should;
It is not enough to gaze from without
You must fairly inhabit the wood
That the wood, evermore may inhabit you)

Your eyes will gambol along with the fawn
Dance with the chasing light
Ears will thrill to the liquid fugue of life
And soul? Your soul will calm
In the sanctury of
The deep, mottled, melodic, inhabiting wood

BUTTERFLY

Seeing three leaves in an autumn wood
I fancy I spy a butterfly
A delicate grace that flutters by
In a lifting gift of golden good

Others may see the same three leaves
And yet not spy the butterfly
No butterfly will flutterby
Unless the passerby believes

CHRIST TOWER

Once, He stood atop the tower
Seen by all the islands around
They called Him the Christ of the Caribbean
Not a strange place for the Galilean
For His place is anywhere there can be found
Those who in weakness would call on His power

Still he is not always welcomed there
By those who resent and resist the might
Of one who claims to be the Way
And so, just as fearsome winds today
Rage and rip both word and light
From out of school and public square

A hurricane swept the statue away
The tower remains and from it nod
Vain trees that seem enticed
To believe they should take the place of Christ
That sad mistakinig of nature for God
We do it too, every day

We praise the sunset, adore the bird
Fall in awe of the breadth of the sea
The height of the sky, each spangling star
Nature's miraculous repertoire
"Miraculous" -- and that's the key
Miracles made by Logos, the Word

Of God that was spoken first at creation
The Logos we learned about from John
It remains to this very day
Hurricanes can't blow it away
No, his statue may be gone
But Jesus lives! Jubilation!

ARCHES N.P.

I was brought here this morning by a power
That power impelling me
Toward the scene-to-be-never-forgot
Knew I'm a fan of fingernail moons
And an app informed there would be one this day.
If I would only get there in time

So up the dark and twisting road, racing my headlights
Into the heart of the park
At times, snaking a curve, spying the settling crescent
Near the horizon now, dropping fast
Another curve and again high rock turrets wall me in
Push harder, drive faster
Outrun those headlights or be too late.
Yet another walled-in curve I sweep around
There . . .

<u>Tableau</u>!

Silver sliver of moon as promised
Falling toward the muted flame of predawn light
Setting off the silhouette of Balanced Rock and varied kin
More than my mind can accept.
And at first more than eyes can see
Until finally they dilate and adjust
Whereupon they are treated to a most felicitous surprise
Almost missed -- a tiny (to my tiny eyes)
Pinprick in the blue velvet sky
Just that

Hello, Venus

Thank you, Power

SUN HALO

So it is called
I do not fully understand
The meteorological causations
Nor want to

Some things
Especially things
With halos
I simply accept
With gratitude and joy

Come Sit with Me at Sunrise

I once wrote a poem:
"Come Sit With Me at Sunset"
About our lives, the two of us
About our some-day deaths, the two of us
About our always, both then and now
Being blessed to be together

In the partnering photograph three chairs stood
I was several times asked, Was the third for Jesus?
Engaging thought (that had not been mine)
In the picture here are two chairs alone
(Jesus now within us?)
And it is the rise not setting of sun
Hence:

"Come sit me at sunrise."
One more sunrise given to us
They grow more precious, each, do they not?
Each an alleluia, some a challenge, even a test
But always Alleluia!

What will this new day offer us?
What will it demand?
I'm glad we don't know
If we knew, how trite would be life
In routine we do not grow
And regardless the calendar
We still are creatures created to grow
Grow in ourselves, of ourselves, though never by ourselves
He of the unseen chair is always accompanying

Let us take this floridly forthcoming day
And challenged by the beauty of this sunrise
Let us make the day it heralds even more glorious
You and I

And Him

Alpenglow

It lasts for only a moment before it is gone
A moment so rare
So briefly sublime
That you have to be there
At just the right time
Or you'll miss the ephemeral magic of alpenglow dawn

No. Not magic. Blessing. A gilded glow
Of lighting and lift
By such a gift
I am moved to extol
The gracious Gifter I need not see to know

The only thing I really need to see
Is the alpenglow
Illuminating
Peaks of snow
And replicating
In the pond, reflected majesty

A sight I wish would never pass away
But the aura of gold
Will unfailingly flee
With me left to hold
But the memory
Of golden mountaintops that taught me how to pray

Perspective I

Do you find yourself sometimes jealous a bit?
You're on an airplane, peering obliquely out
Through a porthole, scratched
At the fortunate folk down there in the heart
Of nature's majesty,
God's gifted glory,
While you, alas, are cocooned and bound
Up here?

Do you find yourself sometimes jealous a bit
To look up, squinting into the burning sun-sky
At the contrail of travelers aloft?
They see it all, from up there, surveying the spread
Of nature's majesty,
God's gifted glory,
While you, alas, are wingless and bound
Down here?

Perspective II

Cow in the field, one side of the wire;
On the other a photographer.
Between the two, a questioning voice.

"You there, animal I see,
Why are you standing there staring at me?
Who are you?
Are you bound somewhere?
If so, whither, whence?
Or are you, as I, simply bound by this fence?
Meant, I guess, to keep one of us in
And one of us out.

Why?
Why would anyone want to keep you
And your camera out?"

Mormon Barn

To see it today is to think of it yesteryear
Viewing in sepia how it was
When still it was called The Hole
Imagine when not just the land around
And mountains beyond
Were wild but the people too
Dissolute, wicked
Notorious sinners and profaners
The dregs
Settled to the bottom of The Hole

But then came a different people
Who built their barns and lives upright
Mormon Barns, they still are called
Reminders of the time The Hole
Was nudged by newcomers just a bit toward
Holy

Reminding that
A simple pinch of the yeast of belief
Can raise an entire loaf

Imagine

Imagine those who faced this parched desert scrub
Knowing if they were to reach their appointed destination
They must first cross miles beyond their reckoning of this
Imagine

And it was hot, it was very, very hot.
As they, in wagons, on foot, astride their beasts of burden
Drove themselves forward
Were driven forward by allure indescribable
Imagine

They were given to see, as visions enticed
What sort of hope might lay ahead
But they did not need those visions
For they had, already, a promise
Burned not on sands or in sun-blaze skies
But burnt ineradicably in their hearts

Inscribed by the spirit that led them now
On an exodus they would never have dared undertake
Alone.
But dare it they did

Imagine

Lunacy

When the desert moon becomes a lollipop
When angels waltz on the head of a pin
When red means go and green says stop
Will I remember?

When I drive on a parkway and park in a drive
When I hear that Munch has painted a grin
When bees forget where they put the hive
I think I'll remember

When desert shivers; Arctic realms sweat
When Vegas decides to give up sin
And pay off every single bet
I'm sure I'll remember

When the mockingbird can't remember a tune
When the Captain of Mensa flunks a quiz
When a lollipop becomes the moon --

Wait!
I remember
It is

OUCH!

It warned.
It always warned
All those years, to all those people
Motoring past old barns of our land
It delivered its caution
Albeit oblique
Coyly secreted within its own name
Such that most would fail to see

Today, the barns are blighted,
Their skins erupting, peeling,
Like tissue of throat or mouth
After too much dip or chew.

Abandoned old barns cry the pain
Of coded warnings, unheeded

Sunrise Psalm

Arriving at a gilded moment
On this sweet Myakka morn
I see a heron in silhouette
Watching the colors of faith reborn

And I worry. Can the bird perceive those colors?
Or does he see them as I now see
Him, in colorless monochrome
What a pity that would be

To be given a sight but not the sight
To see it and appreciate
The gift and, even more, the Gifter
On this puzzle I meditate

But in vain. For back home I discover
That a bird sees colors even better than we
So with no need to pity, I turn to envy
For what every morning this bird gets to see

While I, only occasionally
Ah, but I have a blessing conferred
For I get to see not only the sunrise
But also himself, that silhouette bird

Abstractions

"What is that? Where?"
The questions can annoy an artist
Who knows not how to reply
To answer "A photograph," and "There on the wall"
Would be cynical and rude
But to specify the item pictured
To give a fixed location
Irrelevant, tiresome

Abstraction is left or made abstract for cause
So that each one looking upon it
Can do his own exegesis
Produce her own translation
One should never study only the surface of art
But climb up, crawl in, look around, discover
The message of any art
Is not what the artist puts in
But what the looker, crawler, discoverer, exegete
Brings out

Never think of artist as creator
There's already one of those

HEART TO HEART

Volunteers work hard on Florida beaches
To help what some call "only turtles" survive
Amazing sea turtles. Love and labor each is
Given to keep the threatened species alive

Volunteers giving themselves in what they deem
This worthy cause one day were elated
To find that one mother turtle, so it would seem
Acknowledged and in her way reciprocated

ONLY TURTLES?

Much like hatchling turtles are we
Maneuvering sand
Of an unknown land
Following light
Through dark of night
Scampering toward our destiny

We go by instinct if not always by thought
Surrounded by others
Sisters and brothers
And yet alone
Each on his own
Ready to learn whatever be taught

What impels us at this urgent hour
We do not know
And yet we go
Irresistibly drawn
Toward a distant dawn
By a life-giving, life-taking, life-saving power

Horses Home

It's the time of horses home
They've had a day of frolic and play
Of gallop away
But not to stay
Now, at the end of their frivoling day
Free as the wind to roam
It's the time of horses home

Home that they
May have their hay
And whinny and neigh
As though to say
"Where's that curry comb
It's good to be horses home"

Some day, some day
Our Lord will say
It's the time of Believers home
All saints who would pray
Their failings away
The commands that they
Didn't always obey
Still at end of day
When near the gloam
Will be the time of Believers home

Home to say
Hooray, hooray!
And they will pray
All night and day
Cantabile
To the radiant Ray
'Neath heaven's dome

How good it will be to be Believers home

And Finally . . .

Selah!

The word in scripture seems a direction
To stop, take a break, pause for reflection
Woes of the world shake your *Sangfroid?*
Drowning in blah-blah-blah-blah-blah?

Selah!

Do you feel you are being mediabused?
Harangued, harassed and over-newsed?
Assailed by wars and *coups d'etat?*
Hollywood's latest *menage a trois?*

Selah!

Constantly traveling, too much on the go?
Montreal to Mexico
Then Omaha and Ottawa
And New Orleans for Mardi Gras

Selah!

Society's whirlwind have you agog
Relentlessly chasing the *nouvelle vague*
Dashing from clubhouse to jeweler to spa
Then off to a dinner of quail and *foies gras*

Selah!

Go to the book, open the Psalms
Let poems of David calm your qualms
When you find yourself down to your last hurrah
You need that word from the ancient patois

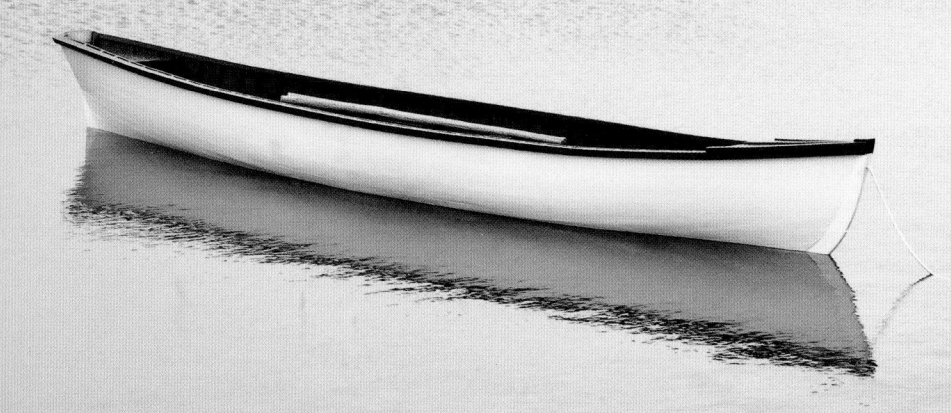

Selah!

Gear & Locations

Most of the photographs here were made on either a kit of Canon camera and lenses; or a Phase One medium format back with Zeiss lenses; or most recently Leica digital cameras and lenses. (One -- guess which -- on an Apple iPhone.)

All were processed and edited through Adobe Lightroom, various versions, with further work done as well with Adobe Photoshop.

Page layouts composed by the artist through Adobe InDesign, the book assembled and printed through the good offices of Four Colour Print Group, Louisville, KY. Printed in China.

Copies can be acquired through "orders@jackperkins.com"

For any curious about the where's of various images, here is a listing by the poem accompanying a photograph. (Didn't want to foul pages by obtrusive page numbers.)

Zarathustra Moment	Apalachicola, FL
Morning Bird	Useppa Island, FL
Honeymoon Cottage	Cedar Key, FL
The First Step	Useppa Island, FL
Eye of the Sky	Ellijay, GA
People of the Steeple	Ellijay, GA
Simple Church	The Palouse, WA
Then and Now	Twillingate, Newfoundland
Homonymic Homily	Grand Teton N.P.
Unbeliever Speaks	Curacao
Parable	Useppa Is. FL
Cold	Two Tops Mt., Idaho
Sperm Whale	Off Newfoundland
Cunningham Cabin	Grand Teton, N.P.
Old Boards	Gilmer County, GA
Ritzy Reflections	Sarasota, FL
Reaching	Olympic N.P.
Kneeling Tree	Apalachicola, FL
Ovation	Dryman Bay, FL
Omigod!	Grand Teton, N.P.
Too Perfect	The Palouse, WA
Psalm of the Rolling Fields	"
Everyday	"
Rape	"
The Gaudy / The Godly	Chimayo, NM
Various Desert Shots	Canyonlands N.P.
	Arches N.P.
Jackstraws	Mt. St. Helens, WA
Bison, Bison, Bison	Jackson Hole, WY
Butterfly	Dingman's Ferry, PA
Christ Tower	St. John, V.I.
Come Sit With Me	Lake MacDonald, MT
Alpenglow	Grand Teton N.P.
Mormon Barn	Jackson Hole, WY
Imagine	Capitol Reef N.P.
Ouch!	Layton, NJ
Sunrise Psalm	Myakka State Park, FL
Horses Home	Private Ranch in Wyoming